Letts

KS1

VISUAL
REVISION
GUIDE

SUCCESS

Mathematics

Author

Paul Broadbent

CONTENTS

NUMBERS

CALCULATIONS

GRAPHS AND CHARTS

MEASURES AND SHAPES

TEST, ANSWERS AND GLOSSARY

CONTENTS

COUNTING OBJECTS

Counting is a really important part of maths – and grouping is a quick way of counting objects.

Count this set of shells.
Make sure you don't miss any out.

Did you count 20 shells?
Now count them in twos: 2, 4, 6, 8...

This can be a lot quicker.
You might even be able to count in groups of five: 5, 10, 15, 20...

COUNTING PATTERNS

COUNTING TO 100

You need to know the numbers to 100.

Use this 100-square to help you learn the positions of all the numbers.

Remember that 34 is 30 + 4 and 67 is 60 + 7.
So to find 67 go down to 60 and then across to 67.

0	1	2	3	4	5	6	7	8	9
10	11	12	13	14	15	16	17	18	19
20	21	22	23	24	25	26	27	28	29
30	31	32	33	34	35	36	37	38	39
40	41	42	43	44	45	46	47	48	49
50	51	52	53	54	55	56	57	58	59
60	61	62	63	64	65	66	67	68	69
70	71	72	73	74	75	76	77	78	79
80	81	82	83	84	85	86	87	88	89
90	91	92	93	94	95	96	97	98	99

To help me get to sleep, I count sheep jumping over a fence.

Whenever I try that, the sheep fall asleep before I do!

SEQUENCES

A <u>sequence</u> is a list of numbers with a pattern.
They are often numbers written in order.

7	8	9	10	11

43	42	41	40	39

If you are asked to write missing numbers from a sequence, look carefully at the numbers you are given. Try to work out the numbers next to these first and then fill out the others.

27	28			31	

29 follows 28, then the next number is 30. Which number follows 31?

TOP TIP

To help you work out the missing number, draw 'jumps' between each number and write the differences.

NUMBER PATTERNS

You can count patterns in many different steps. Look at these jumps in 2s, 5s and 10s:

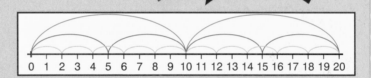

You might be asked to write the next number in a sequence. To work out the steps, look at the difference between the numbers.

QUICK TEST

Work out the missing numbers in these sequences:

1. 28, 29, 30, ___, ___, 33
2. 17, 19, 21, ___, 25, ___
3. 5, 10, ___, 20, ___
4. 90, 80, ___, 60, ___

ANSWERS: 1. 31, 32 2. 23, 27 3. 15, 25 4. 70, 50

HAVE A GO ...

Play the following game with a friend:
• Place buttons to cover different numbers on the 100-square.
• Try to work out what the hidden numbers are.

TEEN NUMBERS

It is easy to get in a muddle with the numbers between 10 and 20. You say them in a different way to the other numbers, so read these and make sure you know how to say each one:

11	eleven	14	fourteen	17	seventeen
12	twelve	15	fifteen	18	eighteen
13	thirteen	16	sixteen	19	nineteen

BIG NUMBERS

2-DIGIT NUMBERS

All our numbers are made from ten <u>digits</u>:

0	1	2	3	4	5	6	7	8	9

The position of these digits in a number makes each number different.

53 Fifty-three
This is 5 'tens' and 3 'ones'.

Tens Ones

72 Seventy-two
This is 7 'tens' and 2 'ones'.

Tens Ones

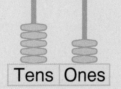

My Gran acts like a teenager.

Yes – she is 71 but pretends she is 17!

TOP TIP
When you read a 2-digit number it helps to break it up into tens and ones.

6

MORE OR LESS

Making a number 10 more or 10 less is easy if you understand how numbers work.

For all these just the 'tens' change.

10 more than 49 is 59
10 less than 84 is 74
10 more than 236 is 246
10 less than 462 is 452

3-DIGIT NUMBERS

Look at these numbers and how they are made:

271 two hundred and seventy-one.

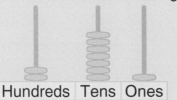

Hundreds | Tens | Ones

649 six hundred and forty-nine.

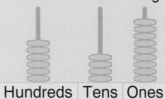

Hundreds | Tens | Ones

The position of a digit in a number is really important. 125 and 512 use the same digits but they are very different numbers. Always check where you put each digit when you write numbers.

Example:
Which different numbers can you make from the digits 3, 6 and 4?
463, 634, 346 are three numbers. Can you find three more?

QUICK TEST

1. Which number comes after fourteen? Is it 51, 15 or 41?

2. What number is this?

Hundreds | Tens | Ones

3. Which number is ten more than 263?

4. Which number is ten less than 487?

ANSWERS: 1. 15 2. 145 3. 273 4. 477

HAVE A GO ...

Go on a number hunt. Look around the house and in newspapers and write down all the numbers you can find. Which is the biggest number you can find?

SPECIAL NUMBERS

ZERO THE HERO

0 is a special number with many names: zero, nothing, nought and nil.

Zero is used in different ways:

This poor leopard has lost all his spots. He has 0 spots.

This number line starts with 0:

0 1 2 3 4 5 6

10, 20, 30, 40, 50 ... all end in 0 – but they are big numbers.

If you have to add zero to a number or take away zero from a number, remember that the number doesn't change.

$$4 + 0 = 4 \qquad 6 - 0 = 6$$

I know 1 is an odd number, because I can't put this sock into a pair.

Yes, you're right – that is an odd sock!

ODD AND EVEN NUMBERS

These are the odd and even numbers to 20.

Remember: odd numbers always end in 1, 3, 5, 7 or 9, and even numbers always end in 0, 2, 4, 6 or 8.

Even numbers can be divided by 2 and odd numbers cannot be divided by 2.

Odd numbers			Even numbers		
1	3	5	2	4	6
7	9	11	8	10	12
13	15	17	14	16	18
	19			20	

MULTIPLES

It is useful to be able to recognise <u>multiples</u> of 2, 5 and 10.

Look at this 100-square to see what is special about these numbers.

Multiples of 2: end in 0, 2, 4, 6, 8.
       of 5: end in 0 or 5.
     of 10: end in 0.

What do you notice about the multiples of 10 on the 100-square?
They are also multiples of both 2 and 5.

1	2	3	4	5	6	7	8	9	10
11	12	13	14	15	16	17	18	19	20
21	22	23	24	25	26	27	28	29	30
31	32	33	34	35	36	37	38	39	40
41	42	43	44	45	46	47	48	49	50
51	52	53	54	55	56	57	58	59	60
61	62	63	64	65	66	67	68	69	70
71	72	73	74	75	76	77	78	79	80
81	82	83	84	85	86	87	88	89	90
91	92	93	94	95	96	97	98	99	100

A DOZEN

Did you know … ?
A <u>dozen</u> is a special number – it means 12.
So now you know how many eggs are in a dozen.

TOP TIP

Remember that even numbers are all multiples of 2.

QUICK TEST

1. Is 27 an even or odd number?

2. If I had a dozen cream cakes and I ate 12 of them, how many would I have left?

3. Is 70 a multiple of 10?

4. Which number between 15 and 25 is a multiple of both 2 and 5?

HAVE A GO …

Write down:
- **3 odd numbers greater than 50**
- **3 multiples of 2**
- **3 multiples of 5**
- **3 multiples of 10.**

ANSWERS: **1.** Odd **2.** Zero (and a tummy ache!) **3.** Yes **4.** 20

FIRST THINGS FIRST

You may have seen numbers with 'st', 'th', 'rd' or 'nd' written after them. These strange endings show the order or position of things. Look at these and try to remember each one:

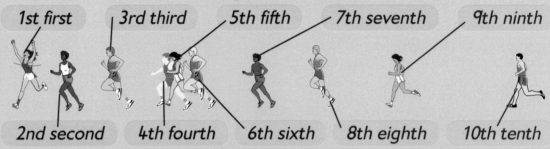

1st first   3rd third   5th fifth   7th seventh   9th ninth

2nd second   4th fourth   6th sixth   8th eighth   10th tenth

GET IN ORDER!

COMPARING NUMBERS

When you need to compare two numbers you must look carefully at the <u>digits</u>. You might be asked to find the biggest or smallest.

For example, which is bigger, 36 or 63?

| 36 is the same as 30 + 6 | 63 is the same as 60 + 3 | 63 is bigger than 36 |

HALFWAY NUMBERS

You might be asked to find a number between two others. For example, what number is halfway between 9 and 13?

This is quite tricky to do in your head – so a good way of working it out is to draw a number line.

9 10 (11) 12 13

ORDERING NUMBERS

When you put numbers in order of size, sort out the 'tens' to start with and then sort the 'ones'.

For example, put these numbers in order, starting with the smallest.

47, 36, 18, 42, 29.

Use these two simple steps:

1st step:
Just look at the 'tens' and write them in order:
18, 29, 36, 47, 42

2nd step:
If any of the 'tens' are the same, put the 'ones' in order:
18, 29, 36, 42, 47

TOP TIP

If you find it difficult to put numbers in order, look carefully at a 100-square, put it away and then try to picture where the numbers are on the square.

NUMBER TRACKS

100 squares, number lines and number tracks are very useful for helping to learn the order of numbers.

1 2 3 4 5 6 7 8 9 10 11 12 13 14 15 16 17 18 19 20

QUICK TEST

1. The first bead is yellow. What colour is the fifth bead?

2. Which number is the biggest: 54 or 45?

3. Which number is halfway between 6 and 14?

4. Write these numbers in order starting with the smallest: 38, 32, 24, 19, 27.

ANSWERS: 1. Blue 2. 54 3. 10 4. 19, 24, 27, 32, 38

HAVE A GO ...

Make a set of digit cards 1 to 9. Choose any three cards.
- Write down all the different numbers you can make. For example with 3, 6 and 2 you can make 26, 63, 3, 263 ...
- Now write them in order.

EASY ESTIMATION

GOOD ESTIMATES

<u>Estimating</u> is a bit like *guessing*. It is better than a guess though – particularly if you are good with numbers.

Have a quick look at this pile of buttons. Without counting, estimate <u>approximately</u> how many buttons there are.

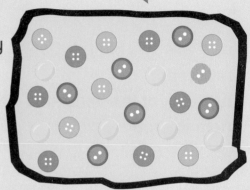

Now count them. There are 25 altogether – but your estimate would be good if you thought there was anything between 20 and 30. An estimate does not need to be exact. It is a good idea to *roughly count them in groups of 5 or 10* – you can do this quite quickly.

Try this with handfuls of buttons or counters and see how good your estimates are.

How far can a dog run into a wood?

NUMBER LINES

You might be asked to estimate the *position of a point on a line*. For example, estimate the whole number marked by the arrow.

```
      ↓
0                    10
├────────────────────┤
```

The best way to do this is to find the *approximate halfway position*. You can then count on to work out the number. So the arrow is just past the middle number which is 5, so it points to the number 6.

Halfway! If it keeps going, it's running out of the wood!

12

ROUNDING

Rounding a number to the nearest ten is useful for estimating.
A round number is a number ending in zero: 10, 20, 30, 40, 50, 60, 70, 80, 90 or 100.

Rounding is easy if you follow these two simple rules:

To round to the nearest 10 look at the 'ones' digit:
1. If it is 5 or more, round up the tens digit.
2. If it is less than 5, the tens digit stays the same.

54 rounds down to 50
38 rounds up to 40
65 rounds up to 70

The halfway numbers like 65, 45, 85, 25 … always round up to the next ten.

TOP TIP

Remember, a number is always between two possible 'round' numbers – you just have to choose which one it's nearest to.

HAVE A GO ...

Play an estimating game in pairs.
- One player takes a handful of buttons or beads and gives an estimate of the number taken.
- The other player says 'higher' or 'lower', if they think the actual number is different from the estimate.
- Count the buttons to find the winner.
- Swap over and repeat the game.

QUICK TEST

```
        A           B
0       ↓           ↓      20
|-------+-----------+------|
```

1. What number is the arrow A pointing to?
2. What number is the arrow B pointing to?
3. What is 74 rounded to the nearest 10?
4. What is 45 rounded to the nearest 10?

ANSWERS: 1. 8 2. 17 3. 70 4. 50

FRIENDLY FRACTIONS

WHAT IS A FRACTION?

A <u>fraction</u> is *part of a whole.*

$\frac{1}{4}$ means 1 part taken out of 4 equal pieces.

So if you want to eat $\frac{1}{4}$ (one quarter) of a pizza, you can cut the pizza into four pieces and take one of the pieces. This leaves $\frac{3}{4}$ (three quarters) for somebody else.

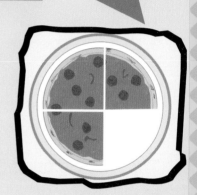

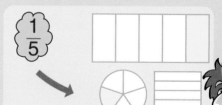

TOP TIP
The bottom number of a fraction shows the number of equal parts.

FRACTIONS OF SHAPES

Try to learn these different fractions:

Did you know that two halves make a whole?

Wow - I'd better be careful that I don't fall into it!

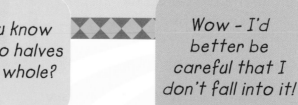

EQUAL PARTS

Look at this shape. Do you think it is divided into *four quarters*?

No, they are not quarters. It is in four parts but the *parts are not equal*. Shapes cut in quarters are in *four equal parts*.

FRACTIONS OF AMOUNTS

It is easy to find $\frac{1}{2}$ or $\frac{1}{4}$ of different amounts, as long as you know how to <u>divide</u>.

Here are 12 sweets.

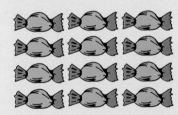

To find $\frac{1}{2}$ of 12, divide the sweets into two equal groups and count one of the groups. So $\frac{1}{2}$ of 12 = 12 ÷ 2 = 6.

To find $\frac{1}{4}$ of 12, divide the sweets into four equal groups and count one of the groups. So $\frac{1}{4}$ of 12 = 12 ÷ 4 = 3.

QUICK TEST

1. What fraction of this square is red?

2. Is this circle divided into halves?

3. What is $\frac{1}{2}$ of 10?

4. What is $\frac{1}{4}$ of 8?

ANSWERS: 1. $\frac{1}{4}$ 2. No 3. 5 4. 2

HAVE A GO ...

You will need a pile of coins or buttons. Take a handful and try to find $\frac{1}{2}$ or $\frac{1}{4}$ of the amount by counting them out. Some will be impossible, but write down the ones that you can divide equally. For example, $\frac{1}{2}$ of 6 = 3.

15

ABACUS NUMBERS

MAKING NUMBERS

You need: 5 counters, buttons or pennies.

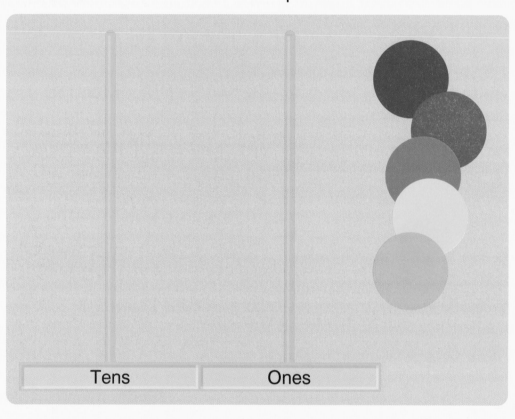

Tens   Ones

❖ Use one counter and place it on the abacus to make different numbers.

   You can make 1 or 10 with one counter.

❖ Which different numbers can you make with two counters? What about 3, 4, 5 … ?

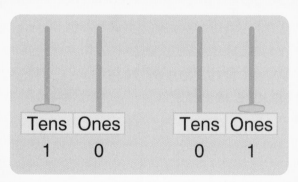

Tens	Ones		Tens	Ones
1	0		0	1

MORE NUMBERS

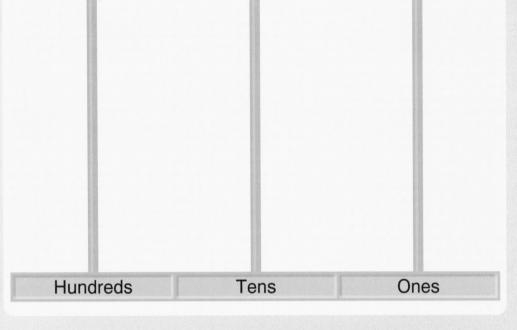

| Hundreds | Tens | Ones |

❖ You can make three different numbers with one counter.

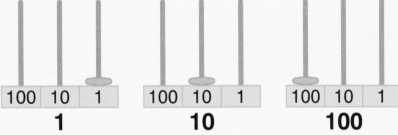

| 100 | 10 | 1 | | 100 | 10 | 1 | | 100 | 10 | 1 |

1   **10**   **100**

❖ How many different numbers can you make with two counters?

What about 3, 4, 5 … ?

Keep a list of all the numbers and write them in order of size.

Hands off, you've spent your pocket money! Ask Mum for some buttons!

Aren't those my pennies?

TEST ROUND-UP

SECTION 1

1. What is the missing number in this sequence?

    38   39   ____   41   42

2. Which number is next after 75?   _____

3. What is the next number in this sequence?

    52   54   56   58   60   ____

4. What number is ten less than 125?   _____

5. 8 − 0 = ?   _____

6. Is 56 an even number or an odd number?   _____

7. Which is bigger, 84 or 48?   _____

8. A box holds a dozen eggs, how many eggs are there?

                                                                 _____

9. Count how many:

    a flowers   _____

    b caterpillars   _____

    c bees   _____

    there are in this picture.

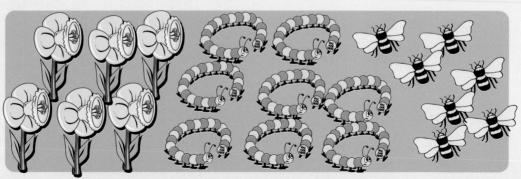

SECTION 2

1. What fraction of each of these shapes is red?

   a   b   c

   _____   _____   _____

2. What number is 10 more than 62?   _____

3. What is 16 rounded to the nearest 10?   _____

4. What number is halfway between 18 and 22?   _____

5. What number between 35 and 45 is a multiple of 10?   _____

6. Is 20 a multiple of both 2 and 5?   _____

7. What number is the arrow pointing to?   _____

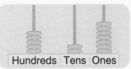

SECTION 3

1. What is $\frac{1}{3}$ of 12?   _____

2. A cake cut into half will be cut into 4 equal pieces.
   True or false?   _____

3. What number is this?   _____

   Hundreds Tens Ones

4. The train is pulling 6 carriages, the first is carrying a horse.

   a Which carriage has an elephant?   _____

   b What animal is in the 5th carriage?   _____

   c What is in the 2nd carriage?   _____

NUMBER FACTS

TOTALS TO 10

Try to learn all these facts for the different <u>totals</u>.
Use these *four steps* to help you:

1. Look at them	2. Cover them up	3. Say the facts	4. Check the facts
0 + 1 = **1**		0 + 7 1 + 6 2 + 5 3 + 4 = **7**	0 + 9 1 + 8 2 + 7 = **9** 3 + 6 4 + 5
0 + 2 1 + 1 = **2**	0 + 5 1 + 4 2 + 3 = **5**		
0 + 3 1 + 2 = **3**			0 + 10 1 + 9 2 + 8 = **10** 3 + 7 4 + 6 5 + 5
0 + 4 1 + 3 2 + 2 = **4**	0 + 6 1 + 5 2 + 4 = **6** 3 + 3	0 + 8 1 + 7 2 + 6 = **8** 3 + 5 4 + 4	

TRIOS

8 − 5 = 3 is a <u>subtraction</u> fact.
The subtraction facts to 10 are easy to remember *if you know your*
<u>addition</u> *facts*.

3 + 5 = 8 and 5 + 3 = 8   These are two addition facts and
you can use them to work out two
subtraction facts: 8 − 5 = 3
8 − 3 = 5

The three numbers 8, 5 and 3 are called
a <u>trio</u>. They can make *four addition*
and subtraction facts.

Think of some more trios and the facts you can make from them.

20

NUMBER BONDS

Try to learn all your <u>number bonds</u> to 20. These are the addition and subtraction facts up to 20, such as 7 + 8, 16 – 9 and so on.

The table below has all the facts. Use it to practise and learn the ones you cannot do quickly.

	0	1	2	3	4	5	6	7	8	9	10
0	0	1	2	3	4	5	6	7	8	9	10
1	1	2	3	4	5	6	7	8	9	10	11
2	2	3	4	5	6	7	8	9	10	11	12
3	3	4	5	6	7	8	9	10	11	12	13
4	4	5	6	7	8	9	10	11	12	13	14
5	5	6	7	8	9	10	11	12	13	14	15
6	6	7	8	9	10	11	12	13	14	15	16
7	7	8	9	10	11	12	13	14	15	16	17
8	8	9	10	11	12	13	14	15	16	17	18
9	9	10	11	12	13	14	15	16	17	18	19
10	10	11	12	13	14	15	16	17	18	19	20

3 + 9 = 12
9 + 3 = 12
12 – 3 = 9
12 – 9 = 3

Close your eyes and count up to 20.

1,2,3,4,5,6,7... and 13 is 20! Coming to find you!

TOP TIP

Remember that 4 + 6 gives the same answer as 6 + 4. It doesn't matter which way round you add.

HAVE A GO ...

- Use number cards 1 to 20 and pick out different trios, such as 4, 5, 9 or 3, 8, 11.
- Write down the four addition and subtraction facts for each trio.

QUICK TEST

Answer these facts as quickly as you can.

1. 3 + 5   **2.** 4 + 6   **3.** 2 + 9   **4.** 4 + 8

5. 7 + 7   **6.** 6 – 4   **7.** 9 – 5   **8.** 11 – 8

9. 14 – 6 **10.** 15 – 11

ANSWERS: **1.** 8 **2.** 10 **3.** 11 **4.** 12 **5.** 14 **6.** 2 **7.** 4 **8.** 3 **9.** 8 **10.** 4

BIG NUMBERS

If you know a fact such as $3 + 6 = 9$, you can use this to work out:

$30 + 60$ $300 + 600$ $3000 + 6000$ (this is getting a bit too big!)

You can also work out $23 + 6$, which is $20 + 3 + 6$.

So you can see that knowing your number bonds to 20 is very useful.

MENTAL MATHS!

USING DOUBLES

Doubles of numbers can be quite easy to work out – so use them to work out other near-doubles.

Examples:
$6 + 6 = 12$ so $6 + 7$ is 1 more, which is 13.
$20 + 20 = 40$ so $20 + 21$ is 1 more, which is 41.

ROUNDING

If you need to add or take away 9, round it to 10 to make it easier.

Examples:
$7 + 9$ 7 add 10, take away 1   Answer: 16.
$14 - 9$ 14 take away 10, add 1   Answer: 5.

You can use this method to add or take away 19, 29, 39, 49 …

ADDING 2-DIGIT NUMBERS

If you need to add two big numbers, it helps to break the numbers up and add the tens, then the ones.

Example:

25 + 37

Use these three steps:

1. Hold the bigger number in your head: 37.
2. Add the tens: 37 + 20 = 57.
3. Add the ones: 57 + 5 = 62.

COUNTING ON

A really good method for a take-away or <u>subtraction</u> is to find the difference between the numbers by counting on.

Example:

34 – 18

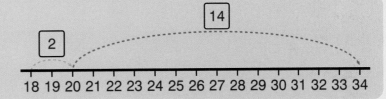

18 19 20 21 22 23 24 25 26 27 28 29 30 31 32 33 34

This number line shows exactly what goes on in your head.

Count on from 18 to 20, then on to 34.

14 + 2 is 16, so 34 – 18 = 16.

HAVE A GO ...

- Take a handful of coins. Work out the total. How much change would there be from 50p or £1?
- Set up a shop. Make some price labels for different items. Make sure you check the totals and give the correct change.

QUICK TEST

Work out the answers to these:

1. 60 + 50
2. The sum of 12 and 13
3. 27 take away 9
4. 16 + 25
5. The difference between 33 and 18

ANSWERS: 1. 110   2. 25   3. 18   4. 41   5. 15

23

MULTIPLYING

COUNTING GROUPS

When you multiply something, you make it larger – and counting groups is a good way of working out a multiplication.

There are 4 fish swimming in each bowl.

How many fish are there altogether in 3 bowls?

3 lots of 4 is the same as 4 + 4 + 4, which is 12. $3 \times 4 = 12$

Remember that the multiply sign (×) means 'lots of' or 'groups of' or 'times'.

Is 3 lots of 4 the same as 4 lots of 3?

The answer is the same, but the fish have a bit more room in their bowls!

If you put the fish together you can see that 4×3 is the same as 3×4.

This is important to remember:

$4 \times 3 = 3 \times 4$
$5 \times 2 = 2 \times 5$
$3 \times 10 = 10 \times 3$

The answers are the same written both ways.

If I divide these 6 sweets between the two of us, I get 4 sweets and you can have 2 sweets.

That's not half! Sharing was never one of your strong points!

DIVIDING

Dividing is the opposite of multiplying – it is the same as sharing or grouping. Both these pictures show 15 divided by 3.

15 shells shared between 3.
There are 5 in each group.
15 ÷ 3 = 5

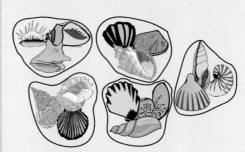

15 shells grouped into 3s.
There are 5 groups.
15 ÷ 3 = 5

Whichever way you look at it, you can see how it fits with multiplying:

3 × 5 = 15   5 × 3 = 15   15 ÷ 3 = 5   15 ÷ 5 = 3

15, 5 and 3 are a special set of three numbers called a <u>trio</u>.

15
5   3

TOP TIP

If you have a division sum to work out, such as 20 ÷ 5, turn it into a multiplication: 5 times something makes 20. If you know your 5× table you can then work it out: 5 × 4 = 20, so 20 ÷ 5 = 4.

HAVE A GO ...

- **Make a multiplying machine.**

IN ×3 OUT
4   12

- **Write numbers on pieces of paper and put them through the machine. Write the answers out.**
- **What happens if you go backwards through the machine?**

QUICK TEST

1. If there are 4 stickers in a packet, how many would there be in 4 packets?

2. Is 3 times 5 the same as 5 times 3?

3. What is double 14?

4. What is half of 12?

5. What is 12 divided by 4?

ANSWERS: 1. 16   2. Yes   3. 28   4. 6   5. 3

25

2 TIMES TABLE

All the numbers in the 2 times table are <u>even numbers</u>. Here is the full set up to 10 × 2:

1 × 2 = 2	
2 × 2 = 4	
3 × 2 = 6	
4 × 2 = 8	
5 × 2 = 10	
6 × 2 = 12	
7 × 2 = 14	
8 × 2 = 16	
9 × 2 = 18	
10 × 2 = 20	

They look easy when they are written in order like this – but you need to know each of these facts *off by heart*.

Write down any that you are not sure of and try to learn them. *Use other facts to help you.*

Example:

* If you can't remember that 6 × 2 is 12, just say 5 × 2 is 10 and 2 more is 12.

TIMES TABLES

MULTIPLYING BY 5 AND 10

These are the easiest tables to learn because of their patterns:

* numbers in the 5 × table always end in 5 or 0.
* numbers in the 10 × table always end in 0.

5 × table	10 × table
1 × 5 = 5	1 × 10 = 10
2 × 5 = 10	2 × 10 = 20
3 × 5 = 15	3 × 10 = 30
4 × 5 = 20	4 × 10 = 40
5 × 5 = 25	5 × 10 = 50
6 × 5 = 30	6 × 10 = 60
7 × 5 = 35	7 × 10 = 70
8 × 5 = 40	8 × 10 = 80
9 × 5 = 45	9 × 10 = 90
10 × 5 = 50	10 × 10 = 100

Do you notice that when it is 5 times an *odd number* the answer *ends in 5*, and when it is 5 times an *even number* the answer *ends in 0*?

Look at these and cover each answer up with your finger. Are there any that you don't know really quickly?

MULTIPLYING BY 3 AND 4

1 × 3 = 3	1 × 4 = 4
2 × 3 = 6	2 × 4 = 8
3 × 3 = 9	3 × 4 = 12
4 × 3 = 12	4 × 4 = 16
5 × 3 = 15	5 × 4 = 20
6 × 3 = 18	6 × 4 = 24
7 × 3 = 21	7 × 4 = 28
8 × 3 = 24	8 × 4 = 32
9 × 3 = 27	9 × 4 = 36
10 × 3 = 30	10 × 4 = 40

These are a bit trickier and there may be some you don't know. Don't panic – use the facts you do know to help learn the others.

Examples:

▼ 8 × 3 is <u>double</u> 4 × 3.

▼ 9 × 3 is 3 less than 10 × 3, so it is 27.

▼ 7 × 4 is double 7 × 2. Double 14 is 28.

TOP TIP

Remember that 2 × 6 gives the same answer as 6 × 2 – it doesn't matter which way round it is written.

TRICKY TABLES

These are the facts for the tables that probably cause the most problems:

6 × 3	7 × 3	9 × 3	6 × 4	8 × 4	9 × 4	8 × 3	7 × 4

Learn one fact a day. **Try this: every time you go through a doorway** at home, *say the fact out loud.*

QUICK TEST

Answer these as quickly as you can:

1. 4 × 3
2. 6 × 5
3. 7 × 10
4. 4 × 4
5. 2 × 9
6. 5 × 4
7. 8 × 4
8. 3 × 10
9. 7 × 2
10. 9 × 3

ANSWERS: 1. 12 **2.** 30 **3.** 70 **4.** 16 **5.** 18 **6.** 20 **7.** 32 **8.** 30 **9.** 14 **10.** 27

HAVE A GO ...

Ask someone to give you a tables test.
• Write 20 tables facts down on paper to read out.
• Record your time and score.
• Try to beat your best time and score.

PUZZLING PROBLEMS

WORD PROBLEMS

Many test questions are disguised as tricky word problems. When you see one, don't panic, just follow the four steps.

Example:
A pet shop has 15 hamsters for sale. On Monday 3 hamsters are sold, and on the following day another 5 hamsters are sold. How many hamsters does the shop still have to sell on Wednesday?

Step 1: Read the problem.
Try to picture the problem and imagine it in real life.

Step 2: Sort out the calculations.
It is 15 take away 3 and then take away another 5.

Step 3: Answer the calculations.
15 − 3 = 12   12 − 5 = 7

Step 4: Answer the problem.
Look back at the question – what is it asking?

Answer: There are 7 hamsters left for sale.

MONEY TOTALS

When you are finding totals of a set of coins, always start with the highest-value coins first. Then you can add the smallest coins.

Example:
Find the total:
50p + 20p +10p + 2p + 2p + 1p = 85p

I'm going to try to save my pocket money this week.

I try to every week - but I think I've got a hole in my pocket!

GIVING CHANGE

When shopkeepers give change, they count on from the price of the item up to the amount of money given.

Examples:

This card costs 37p.
What change will there be from 50p?

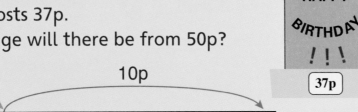

37 38 39 40 41 42 43 44 45 46 47 48 49 50

37p up to 38p is 1p

38p up to 40p is 2p

40p up to 50p is 10p

So the change given is 1p + 2p + 10p, which is 13p.

Try this method giving change from £1.

TOP TIP

Remember that the £ is a 'pound' sign and the 'point' in £4.59 separates the pounds (£4) from the pence (59p). Be careful with zeros: £2.05 means £2 and 5p and £2.50 means £2 and 50p.

QUICK TEST

1. There are 12 tennis balls to put in some tubes. If 3 balls fit in each tube, how many tubes are needed?

2. Kim has 25p and Adam has 10p more than Kim. How much have they got altogether?

3. Rhian has three 10p coins, a 50p coin and two 5p coins in her purse. How much has she got in total?

4. A doughnut costs 34p. What change will there be from 50p?

ANSWERS: 1. 4   2. 60p   3. 90p   4. 16p

HAVE A GO ...

Explain to someone:
- **The four steps for solving word problems.**
- **How to give change from £1 for different items. Use coins to demonstrate the shopkeeper's method of counting on to give change.**

COIN ALPHABET

WHAT IT'S WORTH

Coin Alphabet is a game where you replace the letters in words with numbers. This grid tells you what each letter is worth.

1	A	G	M	S	Y
2	B	H	N	T	Z
5	C	I	O	U	
10	D	J	P	V	
20	E	K	Q	W	
50	F	L	R	X	

Sam is worth 1p + 1p + 1p : a total of 3p.

Paul is worth 10p + 1p + 5p + 50p : a total of 66p.

I'm worth 71p ...

MORE TO TRY

Investigate different boy's and girl's names.

- Can you find any names that are worth the same?
  For example, Sam and Amy are both worth 3p.

- Which 4-letter name is worth the most?
  Which is worth the least?

- Which is the most expensive name you can find?

- Can you find any names that are worth exactly £1?
  Could you find two names that total £1?

... and I'm only worth 3p!

31

TEST ROUND-UP

SECTION 1

1. What is the difference between 20 and 13? _____

2. 600 + 500 = _____

3. What is the sum of 50 and 51? _____

4. There are 5 pencils in a pack, how many pencils are there in 4 packs? _____

5. $3 \times 8 =$ _____

6. A cat had 8 kittens, 3 were tabby, 1 was white and the rest were black. How many kittens were black? _____

7. What is 12 less than 30? _____

8. $60 \div 10 =$ _____

9. What is the total of these coins? _____

10. How much will these cost to buy:

    a 10 flags _____

    b a bucket and a flag _____

    c a bucket and a spade _____

SECTION 2

1. Take away 9 from 34. _____

2. 26 + 15 = _____

3. Kate has £1, she buys an ice cream for 65p.
   How much money does she have left? _____

4. What is 35 divided by 5? _____

5. What is double 30? _____

6. 4 children divide 20 sweets.
   How many sweets do they each get? _____

7. What is half of 40? _____

8. $3 \times 9 =$ _____

SECTION 3

1. **a** How many bags of crisps are there
   altogether in the multipacks? _____

   b How many chocolate bars in total? _____

   c How many more packets of crisps
   are there than chocolate bars? _____

2. I am thinking of a number. If I subtract 11 the answer is 5.
   What number am I thinking of? _____

33

SORT IT OUT!

VENN DIAGRAMS

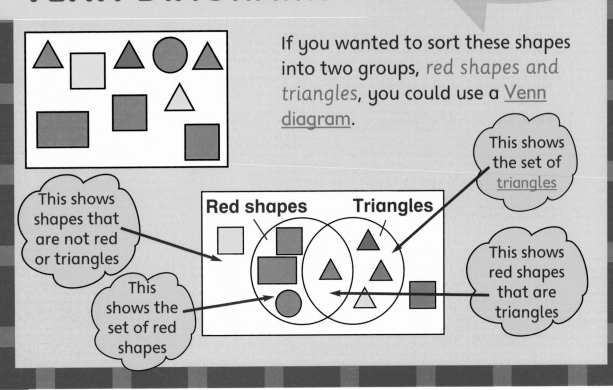

If you wanted to sort these shapes into two groups, *red shapes and triangles*, you could use a <u>Venn diagram</u>.

This shows the set of <u>triangles</u>

This shows shapes that are not red or triangles

This shows the set of red shapes

This shows red shapes that are triangles

Red shapes   **Triangles**

CARROLL DIAGRAMS

Carroll diagrams are very similar to Venn diagrams, except *they use a grid* rather than circles.

You can use a Carroll diagram *to sort numbers.*

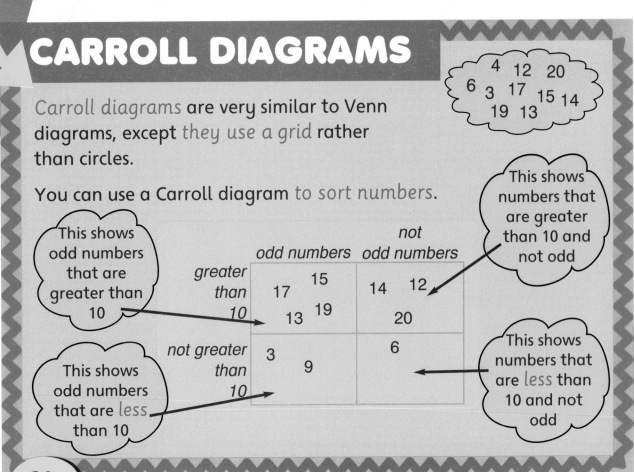

4 12 20
6 3 17 15 14
19 13

This shows numbers that are greater than 10 and not odd

This shows odd numbers that are greater than 10

This shows odd numbers that are *less* than 10

This shows numbers that are *less* than 10 and not odd

	odd numbers	not odd numbers
greater than 10	17 15 13 19	14 12 20
not greater than 10	3 9	6

TREE DIAGRAMS

A tree diagram is a good way of sorting things by asking questions. Each of the answers is either yes or no.

You can use tree diagrams to sort shapes, numbers or objects. This tree diagram sorts some fruit.

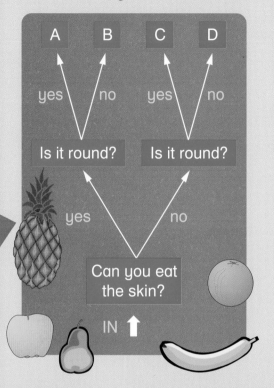

Example:

Start with the banana and follow the questions through the tree diagram.

Can you eat the skin of a banana? No

Is a banana round? No

So a banana ends up in box D.

Which boxes do the other fruits in this section go into?

I wonder if this is called a fruit tree diagram?

I'd rather have a fruit and nut diagram!

QUICK TEST

From this Venn diagram name someone who has:

fair hair	blue eyes
Jo	David
	Laura
	Jordan
Ali	Jack

1. Blue eyes and fair hair

2. Blue eyes but not fair hair

3. Neither fair hair nor blue eyes

4. Fair hair but not blue eyes

HAVE A GO ...

Sort the numbers to 20 in different ways using:

• A Venn diagram
• A Carroll diagram
• A tree diagram.

Compare each of the ways of sorting.

PERFECT PICTOGRAMS

PICTOGRAMS

Pictograms use symbols or pictures, where each symbol represents a certain number of items.

Look carefully at what each picture stands for. Each picture represents 2 jelly babies, so there are 9 purple jelly babies in the box. Count to check.

How many red jelly babies are there? You should have counted 6.

This pictogram shows how many jelly babies are in a box.

Green	🧍🧍🧍
Yellow	🧍🧍🧍🧍▌
Red	🧍🧍🧍
Orange	🧍🧍▌
Pink	🧍▌
Black	🧍🧍🧍🧍

KEY 🧍 = 2 jelly babies

The pictogram below shows the hours of sunshine each week for 6 weeks.

For this pictogram, each sun stands for 5 hours of sunshine. So in week one, there were between 15 and 20 hours of sunshine.

Which week had 33 hours of sunshine? Week 6 is the only week with between 30 and 35 hours of sunshine, so this must be the one.

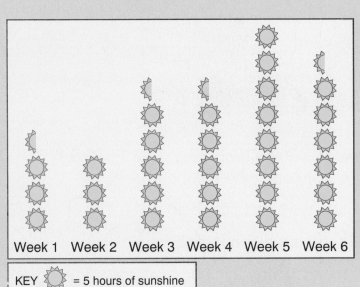

KEY ☀ = 5 hours of sunshine

BLOCK GRAPHS

Block graphs are the easiest type of graph, because *each block shows one thing*. But, as with all graphs, you still need to look at it carefully.

Which is the most popular vegetable? You can see that peas are the most popular: 7 children chose them.

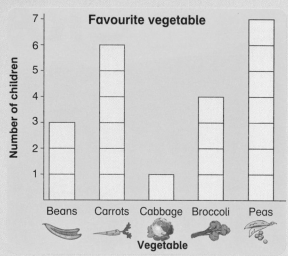

Favourite vegetable

How many more children liked broccoli than cabbage? This is a typical question you may get asked. Work out *both amounts* and then *find the difference*. 4 children liked broccoli, 1 child liked cabbage. 4 – 1 is 3. So the difference is 3.

You can work out how many children were in the group altogether by *counting all the blocks*.

I'm amazed that someone chose yukky cabbage as their favourite vegetable.

Actually it was me! Nicer than your mushy peas!

QUICK TEST

Use the graphs on these pages to answer these questions:

1. How many more black jelly babies are there in the box than green ones?

2. How many hours of sunshine were there in week 2?

3. How many children chose beans as their favourite vegetable?

ANSWERS: 1. 2 more   2. 15 hours   3. 3

HAVE A GO ...

- Carry out a survey of favourite vegetables or fruit with members of your family.
- Draw a pictogram or block graph to show your results.

GROOVY GRAPHS

BAR CHARTS

Information can be shown in many ways using different graphs, and <u>bar charts</u> are a very popular type. To understand bar charts, look carefully at the different parts of this graph.

This graph shows the birds that visited a bird table.

> 1. **Work out the** <u>scale</u> – look carefully at the numbers – do they go up in 1s, 2s, 5s, 10s … ?

> 2. **Read the title** – what is it all about? Is there any other information given?

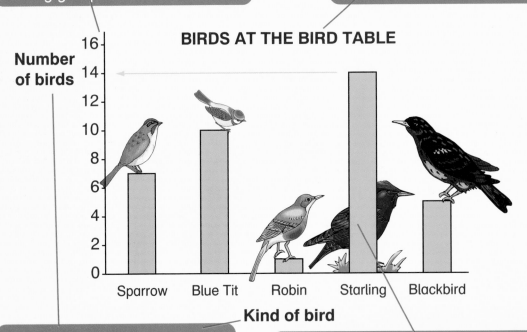

> 3. **Look at the** <u>axis</u> **labels** – these should explain the lines that go up and across

> 4. **Compare the bars** – read them across to work out the amounts.

The scale is very important. This graph goes up in 2s. You can see that the number of sparrows is halfway between 6 and 8 – so there were 7 sparrows visiting the bird table.

TOP TIP

Before trying to answer any questions about a graph, spend a little time reading and trying to understand it.

CHANGING SCALES

This graph has a scale that goes up in fives.

Jack measured the height of the flowers in his flowerbed.

Use the graph to check the different heights of the flowers.

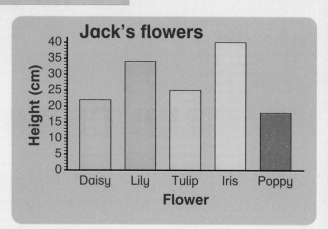

Jack's flowers

You can easily see that the iris is the tallest flower, but you need to *look across carefully to check the height*. It might be a good idea to *use a ruler* to give you a straight line.

> A common test question is something like:
> *How much taller is the lily than the poppy?*

All you need to do is find the height of each flower and work out the difference. The lily is 34 cm and the poppy is 18 cm.

34 – 18 = 16
So the lily is 16 cm taller than the poppy.

It might help if you water them!

I planted some cress last week and I'm going to measure the height each day. The only thing is ... it hasn't grown at all yet.

QUICK TEST

Use the graphs on these pages to answer these questions:

1. How many blackbirds were seen at the bird table?

2. How many more sparrows than robins were seen?

3. Which flower measured 22 cm tall?

4. Which flower is 15 cm shorter than the iris?

HAVE A GO ...

Grow some cress and check its height each day. Draw a bar chart to show the results.

ANSWERS: **1.** 5 **2.** 6 **3.** Daisy **4.** Tulip

39

WHAT'S THE WEATHER?

WEATHER CHART

Use these different diagrams, charts and graphs to record the weather for a week … or longer.

Weather chart for the week

Weather	1	2	3	4	5	6	7
snow							
wind							
rain							
cloud							
sun							

Day

It's great when it's sunny and I can play outside!

SUNSHINE AND TEMPERATURE

Hours of sunshine

Saturday	
Sunday	
Monday	
Tuesday	
Wednesday	
Thursday	
Friday	

Key

☀ = 2 hours

Highest daily temperature

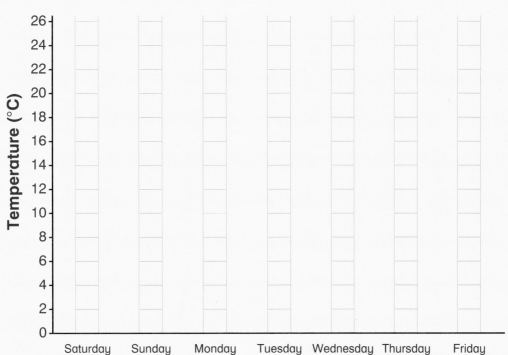

Look at the information you've collected.
What have you found out about the weather?

Yes, it leaves me to read my book in peace!

TEST ROUND-UP

SECTION 1

Types of pets owned by class 2B.

1. How many children have rabbits? _____

2. Which pet is the most popular? _____

3. How many children have birds? _____

4. How many more children have dogs than cats? _____

Types of pets owned by Class 2B

(bar chart: rabbit 8, cat 5, hamster 10, dog 7, bird 0, fish 3; y-axis "Number of children" 0–10; x-axis "Type of pet")

This survey shows favourite types of sandwich fillings.

5. What does one sandwich symbol represent? _____

6. How many children chose tuna sandwiches? _____

7. Which type of sandwich was chosen by 5 children?

   _____

8. Which was the most popular sandwich? _____

Sandwich fillings

Filling:	
ham	🍞🍞🍞
cheese	🍞🍞🍞🍞
egg	🍞
tuna	🍞🍞

Key: 🍞 = 2 sandwiches

Look at this Venn diagram.

9. Which creatures can fly but are not birds?

   _____

10. Which birds cannot fly?

    _____

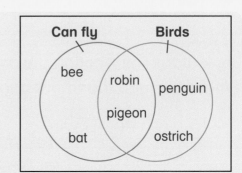

(Venn diagram: "Can fly" — bee, bat; overlap — robin, pigeon; "Birds" — penguin, ostrich)

SECTION 2

Heights

1. Who is the shortest?

   _____

2. How tall is Sanjay? _____

3. What is the difference in height between Hannah and Lucy?   _____

4. Which two children are the same height? _____

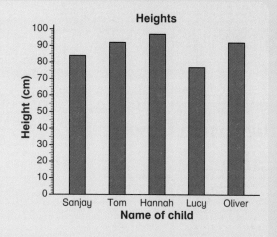

Skipping

5. Who skipped the greatest number of times?_____

6. How many more times did Harry skip than David?

   _____

7. Who skipped the same number of times as Ali?

   _____

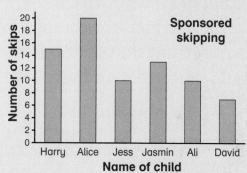

8. What was the total number of skips made by all the children together?   _____

Brothers and sisters

9. Copy this Carroll diagram. Write your name and the names of 6 of your friends in the correct places on this Carroll diagram.

   _____

10. How many children have both brothers and sisters?

    _____

	has brother	no brother
has sister		
no sister		

MEASUREMENT

UNITS OF MEASUREMENT

Length, mass and capacity are all measured using different units. Try to learn these:

Capacity
1 litre (l) = 1000 millilitres (ml)

Mass
1 kilogram (kg) = 1000 grams (g)

Length
1 metre (m) = 100 cm   1 kilometre (km) = 1000 m

It is important to write *the units* in your answers. Which units of measurement do you think would be correct on these labels?

Check your answers by looking in your kitchen cupboards.

TOP TIP

A handspan is about 10 cm long, so use this to work out the approximate length of objects by counting in tens.

I think this bucket holds about 5 litres.

That's just enough to get you absolutely soaked!

HEAVIER OR LIGHTER?

We measure mass using grams and kilograms. To help you get an idea of these masses, look at these. They are all <u>approximate</u> amounts:

1 gram – a pinch of salt	20 grams – a teaspoon of sugar
100 grams – an apple	1000 grams or 1 kg – a bag of sugar

Try to get a feel for these masses by holding different objects and 'weighing' them in your hands.

LONGER OR SHORTER?

We measure the length of objects using a ruler or tape measure, but before you measure something it is a good idea to work out roughly how long it is. This is called <u>estimating</u>.

Example: Is your shoe longer or shorter than 10 cm? You need to know how long 10 cm is to work this out.

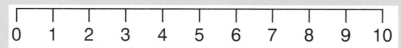

Look at different objects and estimate whether they are longer or shorter than 10 cm. Try comparing objects with 30 cm, 50 cm and 1 metre.

QUICK TEST

1. How many millilitres are there in 1 litre?

2. A door is about 2 metres high. True or false?

3. Approximately how heavy is a pencil – 20 g or 200 g?

4. What is measured in kilograms – length, mass or capacity?

ANSWERS: 1. 1000 ml   2. True   3. 20 g   4. Mass

HAVE A GO ...

Play an estimating game called 'higher or lower'. Choose an object, pick it up and 'weigh' it in your hands. Estimate the mass, then check on the scales to see if you are right.

TELLING THE TIME

TIME FACTS

There are lots of time facts to try to learn.
Cover each one up and see how many you know.

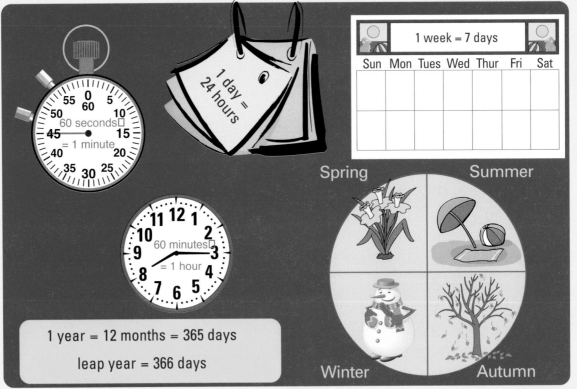

60 seconds = 1 minute

1 day = 24 hours

1 week = 7 days

Sun	Mon	Tues	Wed	Thur	Fri	Sat

60 minutes = 1 hour

1 year = 12 months = 365 days

leap year = 366 days

Spring   Summer   Winter   Autumn

Jan Mar May Jul   Aug Oct Dec
Feb Apr Jun   Sep Nov

Use a 'knuckle method' to learn the days
of the months:

All the 'knuckle months' have 31 days.
February has 28 days (29 days in a leap year)
and April, June, September and November have 30 days.

TOP TIP

Put a calendar up in your bedroom so you can mark off the days for each month. You'll soon get to know the order of the days in the week and the months in the year.

MEASURES AND SHAPES

46

READING THE TIME

We read the time using these two types of clock:

an analogue **clock with hands**

the long hand shows how many minutes past the hour

the short hand shows the hour

a digital **clock with the time shown in numbers**

shows the hour

shows how many minutes past

Both these clocks show 'four fifteen' or 15 minutes past 4.

READING A CIRCULAR CLOCK FACE

If you find it difficult to tell the time, then follow these *three easy steps* and you'll be a 'watch wizard' in no time at all!

1. *Start with the short hour hand* on your clock or watch and look at the last hour that this has gone past. This has gone past the 5, so it is past 5 o'clock.
2. *Look at the longer minute hand* and count around in fives from the top to the hand: 5, 10, 15, 20, 25, 30, 35, 40.
3. *Say aloud the hour followed by the number of minutes* – so you say 5:40, which means 40 minutes past 5.

Simple – now *practise* it with different times, and don't worry, say the times to the nearest 5 minutes until you get the hang of it.

QUICK TEST

1. How many minutes are there in 1 hour?
2. Which day comes after Wednesday?
3. Which month comes before October?
4. What time does this show?

HAVE A GO …

Ask someone to write down a digital time, such as 2:45. Use an old watch or clock and try to make that time by turning the hands.

FLAT SHAPES

SHAPE NAMES

There are lots of mathematical shapes with great names – it's important to *recognise these shapes* and *know their names.*

Number of sides	Name	
3	Triangle	
4	Quadrilateral	
5	Pentagon	
6	Hexagon	
7	Heptagon	
8	Octagon	

TOP TIP

It is useful to remember that some shapes have several different names. A 4-sided shape is called a quadrilateral. Some quadrilaterals are also rectangles or oblongs.

Regular shapes are special shapes with all sides and angles equal.

If you see a shape and don't know its name, just count *the number of sides.*

So this is a *6-sided shape.* It's even better if you remember that it is called a hexagon.

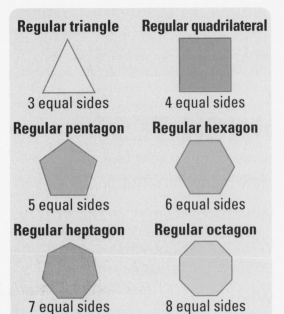

Regular triangle	Regular quadrilateral
3 equal sides	4 equal sides
Regular pentagon	**Regular hexagon**
5 equal sides	6 equal sides
Regular heptagon	**Regular octagon**
7 equal sides	8 equal sides

SORTING SHAPES

A Venn diagram is useful for sorting shapes.

A circle and an oval have one curved side so they are in the outside set.

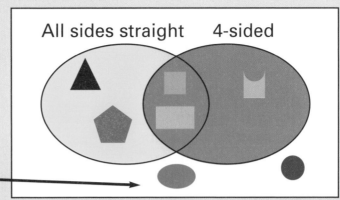

SYMMETRY

Some shapes are symmetrical – they have lines of symmetry. Look at this shape:

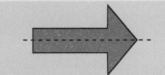

If you imagine it folded down the middle, the two sides would match. That fold line is the line of symmetry and shows that a shape or pattern is symmetrical.

These letters are symmetrical. Can you see where the lines of symmetry would be?

A B C D

HAVE A GO ...

Play a feely bag game with someone.

- Cut out different shapes from card or plastic.
- Put them in a bag and shake them up.
- Feel one of the shapes through the bag and describe it – can the other person name it from your description?

QUICK TEST

1. What is the name of a six-sided shape?

2. How many sides does a pentagon have?

3. Which shape has four equal sides and angles?

4. Is this triangle symmetrical?

ANSWERS: 1. Hexagon 2. 5 3. Square 4. Yes

49

SHAPE NAMES

Solid shapes are all around us and many of them have special names.

Try this: Look at one shape and remember its name.
◆ Close your eyes and picture the shape floating on the back of your eyelids.
◆ Turn the shape around and try to picture it with different parts facing you.
◆ Try this with other shapes so that you really get to know them.

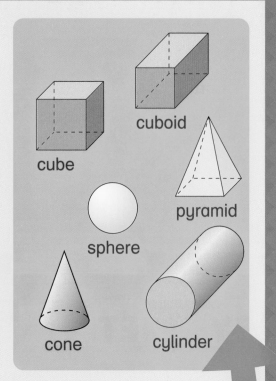

cube
cuboid
pyramid
sphere
cone
cylinder

SOLID SHAPES

PARTS OF SOLID SHAPES

Solid shapes are made up of <u>faces</u>, <u>edges</u> and <u>corners</u>.

A face is a flat surface of a solid.
An edge is where two faces meet.
A corner is where three or more edges meet.

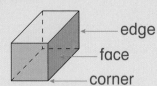

edge
face
corner

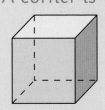

A cube has 6 faces, 12 edges and 8 corners.

A cylinder has 3 faces (2 flat and 1 curved), 2 edges and no corners.
Check the faces, edges and corners of other shapes.

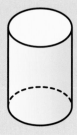

SORTING SHAPES

You can sort shapes using a Carroll diagram.

	pyramid	not a pyramid
one or more square faces	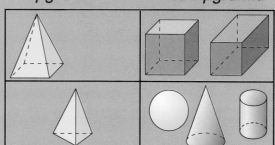	
no square faces		

SHAPES ALL AROUND US

These solid shapes you are learning about make a lot of the shapes that are all around us. It is important to be able to recognise and name the shapes. Go on a shape hunt and see how many cubes, cuboids, spheres, cylinders, cones and pyramids you can find.

I think a cone is my favourite shape.

Me too - with strawberry ice cream!

QUICK TEST

1. Which shape has 6 square faces and 8 corners?

2. How many faces does a cylinder have?

3. What is the name of the shape that is absolutely round like a ball?

4. What is this shape called?

ANSWERS: 1. Cube 2. 3 3. Sphere 4. Pyramid

HAVE A GO ...

• Find some 3D shapes from packets and boxes around the house.
• List the number of faces, edges and corners.

GRIDS

A grid can be used to show the position of something. On this grid the tree is at C3 and the car is at A2. Can you see that you read the letter first, then the number, to give the position?

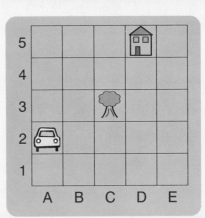

ON THE MOVE

RIGHT ANGLES

Corners of doors, windows, books, tables all show right angles.

These are 'square' angles and can be seen all around us.

A right angle is a quarter turn, clockwise or anticlockwise.

Squares and rectangles have four right angles – one at each corner.

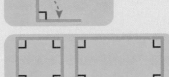

Can you remember the points of the compass?

Yes, I've made up my own saying: Never Empty Smelly Wellies!

DIRECTIONS

Clockwise and anticlockwise are instructions for moving in different directions.

This direction is clockwise.

This is anti-clockwise

Quarter turns, half-turns and whole turns are used to describe how far to turn.

This arrow has moved a quarter turn clockwise.

This arrow has moved a half-turn anticlockwise.

A whole turn is a complete circle. This is a whole turn clockwise.

TOP TIP

Remember, clockwise moves in the direction of clock hands and anticlockwise goes in the opposite direction.

POINTS OF THE COMPASS

It is useful to know the points of the compass.

To remember the order, look at the initials NESW. A well-known saying to learn this order is Naughty Elephants Squirt Water!

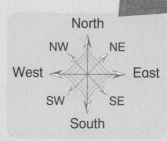

QUICK TEST

1. What position is the car on the grid on page 52?

2. Which compass direction is opposite the west?

3. Which point will the arrow move to if it goes a quarter turn anticlockwise?

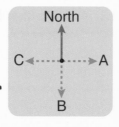

ANSWERS: 1. A2 2. East 3. C

HAVE A GO ...

Set a course for someone to walk through. Use clockwise, anti-clockwise, left, right, quarter turns and half-turns for direction. Use steps for distance.

53

SHAPE PARTS

BUILDING SHAPES

This is a half-shape.

The whole shape could be one of these.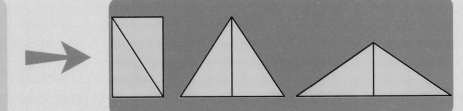

- ♣ Use thin card or paper.
- ♣ Cut out your own 'half-shapes'.
- ♣ Find all the whole shapes that can be made from your half.
- ♣ You could choose one of these half-shapes.

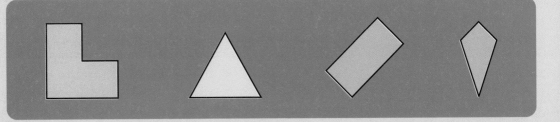

TOP TIP

Keep the starting shape simple and then try to find as many different complete shapes as you can. There may be lots!

BIGGER SHAPES

This is a quarter of a shape.

The whole shape could be one of these.

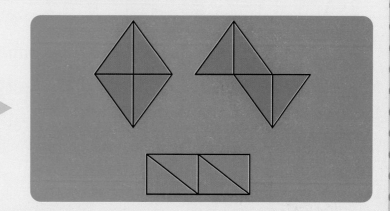

♣ Make your own 'quarter-shapes'.

♣ Find the different whole shapes that you can make from your quarter-shape.

♣ Make a set of whole shapes and glue them on a piece of paper to display them.

I think I have found a quarter of a footprint.

Maybe it was someone walking on tiptoes!

55

TEST ROUND-UP

SECTION 1

1. What is the name of a five-sided shape? _____

2. How many minutes are there in an hour? _____

3. Which shape has three sides and three corners?

   _____

4. Which month comes after July? _____

5. What shape is this? _____

6. How many faces does a cube have? _____

7. What number is opposite 3 on a clock face? _____

8. Is a square symmetrical? _____

9. What is the time on each of these clocks?

   a.    b.    c.

      _____

10. Which of these is a right angle? _____

   a. 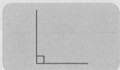   b.   c.

SECTION 2

1. Which compass point is opposite south? _____

2. How much does the parcel weigh?

   _____

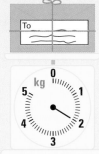

3. What units would you use to measure a glass of orange drink: centimetres, grams or millilitres? _____

4. Measure this line with a ruler.
   Is it nearest to 5 cm, 6 cm or 7 cm? _____

5. A banana is heavier than 1 kg. True or false? _____

6. Which is the same amount as 1 litre?

   10 ml   100 ml   1000 ml

7. If you are facing north and you do a quarter turn clockwise, what direction will you be facing? _____

8. Which object is to the left of the bucket on the grid?

   _____

9. Which object is south of the sandcastle?

   _____

10. Which objects are at
    a. C4 _____
    b. A1 _____
    c. D2 _____?

NATIONAL TEST PRACTICE

1. What number is 10 more than 452? _____

2. What is 4 metres in centimetres? _____

3. What is the next number in this sequence? _____

   17   19   ___   23   25   27

4. November has 31 days. True or false? _____

5. Which solid shape has no corners, 3 faces and 2 round edges?

   _____

6. Which of these angles is a right angle? _____

   a.    b.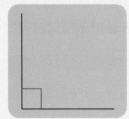

7. 44 + 45 = ? _____

8. What is 6 multiplied by 3? _____

This graph shows how children travel to school.

 = 5 children   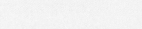 = 1 to 4 children

car	🧍🧍🧍🧍
bus	🧍🧍
walk	🧍🧍
cycle	🧍

9. How many children travel by car? _____

10. Do more children travel by bus or walk? _____

11. 27 ÷ 3 = ? _____

12. How many corners has a sphere? _____

13. Tariq has £1 and he buys a pen for 45p and a rubber for 15p.
How much change will he have? _____

14. Is 20 a multiple of 4? _____

15. Write these numbers in order, starting with the smallest

    37   16   31   19   44 _____

16. How many sides has an octagon? _____

17. Harry needs 18 cakes for his party and there are
4 cakes in a box. How many boxes of cakes will
he need to make sure everyone gets one cake? _____

18. Is 54 an odd or even number? _____

19. Estimate the position of each arrow.

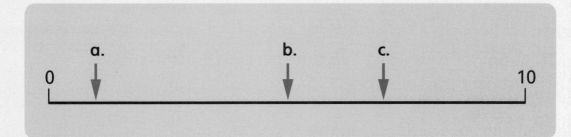

a. _____   b. _____   c. _____

20. What time is shown on each of these clocks?

a. _____   b. _____   c. _____

21. What number is 10 less than 98? _____

22. $7 \times 5 = ?$ _____

23. Which letter will the arrow point to if it moves
a half turn clockwise from the arrow? _____

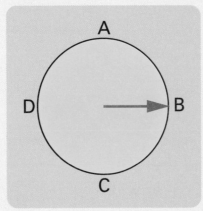

24. How many sides has a hexagon? _____

25. Which number comes after seventeen?
Is it 18 or 81? _____

26. What is 300 cm in metres? _____

27. A pair of shoes cost £35 but there is £9 off in a sale.
What is the sale price ? _____

28. $33 + 34 = ?$ _____

29. Place these numbers correctly on this Venn diagram.

12   4   30   25   15   9   23

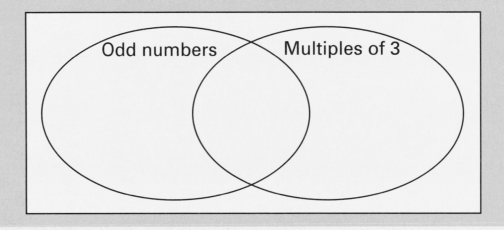

30. Which numbers on the Venn diagram are
multiples of 3 and also even? _____

31. Which day comes before Thursday? _____

32. What is the missing number?

30   35   ____   45   50 _____

33. 53 – 9 = ? _____

34. Jasmin swims 20 m further than Ben.
Ben swims double the distance of Holly.
Holly swims 15 m. How far did Jasmin swim? _____

35. How much juice is in this jug? _____

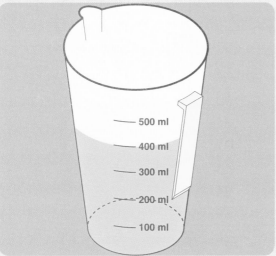

36. What is the largest number that can be made
from the digits 3, 7, and 5? _____

37. Is a teaspoon longer or shorter than 5 cm? _____

38. What position on the compass is opposite west? _____

39. Name each of these shapes.

a. _____   b. _____   c. _____

40. Which shape is not symmetrical, a, b, or c? _____

ANSWERS

NATIONAL TEST PRACTICE ANSWERS

1. 462
2. 400 cm
3. 21
4. False
5. Cylinder
6. b
7. 89
8. 18
9. 20
10. Travel by bus
11. 9
12. None
13. 40p
14. Yes
15. 16   19   31   37   44
16. 8
17. 5
18. Even number
19. a. 1   b. 5   c. 7
20. a. 6.45   b. 11.10   c. 2.30
21. 88
22. 35
23. D
24. 6

25. 18
26. 3 metres
27. £26
28. 67
29.

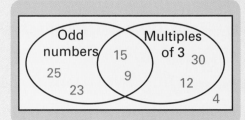

30. 12 and 30
31. Wednesday
32. 40
33 44
34. 50 m
35. 400 ml
36 753
37. Longer
38. East
39. a.   Rectangle
    b.   Circle
    c.   Quadrilateral
40. c

TEST ROUND-UP ANSWERS

Numbers   **pages 18–19**
  Section 1
  1. 40
  2. 76
  3. 62
  4. 115

5. 8
6. An even number
7. 84
8. 12
9. There are:
    a. 6 flowers   b. 8 caterpillars
    c. 7 bees in this picture.

Section 2

1. a. $\frac{1}{3}$ b. $\frac{1}{2}$ c. $\frac{1}{4}$
2. 72
3. 20
4. 20
5. 40
6. Yes
7. 2

Section 3

1. 4
2. False
3. 527
4. a. 4th
   b. Lion
   c. Clown

Calculations   pages 32–33

Section 1

1. 7
2. 1100
3. 101
4. 20
5. 24
6. 4
7. 18
8. 6
9. 43p
10. a. 90p b. 54p c. 95p

Section 2

1. 25
2. 41
3. 35p
4. 7
5. 60
6. 5
7. 20
8. 27

Section 3

1. a. 30   b. 20   c. 10
2. 16

Graphs and charts   pages 42–43

Section 1

1. 8
2. Hamster
3. 0
4. 2
5. 2 sandwiches
6. 4
7. Ham
8. Cheese
9. Bee and bat
10. Penguin and ostrich

Section 2

1. Lucy
2. 84 cm
3. 20 cm
4. Tom and Oliver
5. Alice
6. 8
7. Jess
8. 75

Measures and shapes
pages 56–57

Section 1

1. Pentagon
2. 60
3. Triangle
4. August
5. Square
6. 6
7. 9
8. Yes
9. a. 10.30   b. 1.25   c. 8.50
10. c

Section 2

1. North
2. 2 kg
3. Millilitres
4. 5 cm
5. False
6. 1000 ml
7. East
8. Starfish
9. Crab
10. a. Flag   b. Crab   c. Bucket

GLOSSARY

Addition Adding one amount to another.

Approximate A 'rough' answer – near to the real answer.

Anticlockwise Turning in this direction, opposite to the hands of a clock.

Axis (Plural is axes) The horizontal and vertical lines on a graph.

Bar charts A type of graph that has bars to show amounts.

Block graphs A type of graph where each block means one amount.

Calculation Adding, taking away, multiplying and dividing are all calculations.

Capacity The amount of liquid a container holds.

Clockwise Turning in this direction, like the hands of a clock.

Coins The money we use: 1p, 2p, 5p, 10p, 20p, 50p, £1, £2 are all coins.

Corners Where the edges or sides of shapes meet.

Digits There are 10 digits : 0 1 2 3 4 5 6 7 8 and 9 that make all the numbers we use.

Divide Share or group. ÷ is the sign for divide.

Double Make something twice as big, or multiply by 2.

Dozen Another word for twelve.

Edges Where two faces of a solid shape meet.

Estimate/estimating A good guess.

Even numbers Numbers that can be divided exactly by 2. They end in 0 2 4 6 or 8.

Faces The flat sides of a solid shape.

Fraction Part of a whole one.

Half $\frac{1}{2}$ is one half, or one out of two parts.

Heptagon A shape with 7 straight sides.

Hexagon A shape with 6 straight sides.

Length How long an object is – can be measured in centimetres or metres.

Mass The amount of material that makes up an object.

Multiples A multiple is a number made by multiplying together two other numbers.

Number bonds These are the addition and subtraction facts under 20.

Octagon A shape with 8 straight sides.

Odd numbers Numbers that cannot be divided exactly by 2. Odd numbers always end in 1, 3, 5, 7 or 9.

Pentagon A shape with 5 straight sides.

Pictograms Graphs that use symbols or pictures, where each symbol represents a certain number of items.

Quadrilateral A shape with 4 straight sides.

Right angles A quarter turn. The corner of a square is a right angle.

Rounding Changing a number to the nearest ten. A 'round number' is a number ending in zero: 10, 20, 30, 40, 50, 60, 70, 80, 90 or 100.

Scale These are the labelled marks that show an amount on rulers, jugs and weighing scales.

Sequence A list of numbers which usually has a pattern. They are often numbers written in order.

Square A shape with four equal sides.

Subtraction Taking one amount away from another.

Symmetrical When two halves of a shape or pattern are identical.

Total When you add some numbers, the answer is the total.

Trio A set of three.

Triangle A shape with 3 straight sides.

Venn diagram A diagram that shows groups of things by putting circles around them.

Zero 0 or nothing.